™

SEED *of* DESTRUCTION

HELLBOY

SEED *of* DESTRUCTION

MIKE MIGNOLA ✝ JOHN BYRNE

HELLBOY™

SEED *of* DESTRUCTION

by
MIKE MIGNOLA

Script by
JOHN BYRNE

Miniseries colors by
MARK CHIARELLO

Cover colors by
DAVE STEWART

Short-story colors by
MATTHEW HOLLINGSWORTH

✠

Introduction by
ROBERT BLOCH

Series and collection edited by
BARBARA KESEL *with* SCOTT ALLIE

Hellboy logo designed by
KEVIN NOWLAN

Collection designed by
MIKE MIGNOLA & CARY GRAZZINI

Published by
MIKE RICHARDSON

DARK HORSE BOOKS™

Published by Dark Horse Books
A division of Dark Horse Comics, Inc.
10956 SE Main St.
Milwaukie, OR 97222
www.darkhorse.com

First Edition: October 1994
Second Edition: June 1997
Third Edition: November 2003
ISBN: 1-59307-094-2

This volume collects issues one through four of the Dark Horse comic-book series,
Hellboy: Seed of Destruction, and stories from *San Diego Comic-Con Comics #2* and the *Comics Buyer's Guide*.

10 9 8 7

PRINTED IN CHINA

INTRODUCTION

by ROBERT BLOCH

*I*F SOME-
ONE HAD
TOLD ME
FIFTY YEARS AGO THAT
I'd ever write the introduction to a collection of comics, I'd have told him he was crazy, and that *I* would have to be crazy in order to do so.

Back then I was writing short stories for the pulp magazines. Neither the publications nor the material I sent them was a major contribution to the status of American literature, but by virtue of it I could at least call myself a writer. Today I probably could have made the same claim — and gotten more critical and media attention — if I'd just gone around spraying out *graffiti*. Nevertheless, even though I lacked such opportunities, I was a published writer. Some of my colleagues, equally proud of their status, were less satisfied with their incomes. Under various pseudonyms they moonlighted, turning out scripts and story lines for the comic books. But this was not something one talked about in polite society, nor spoke of in private. Even in those days there were limits to admitting one's indiscretions; anyone might proclaim himself a born-again Christian, but few would admit to being a burn-again Satanist.

And comic books, to some, were satanic. They were gross, sleazy vehicles of violence, and their creators were the kind of people who gave child-molesting a bad name.

So thought Dr. Frederick Wertham, a psychiatrist who launched an attack on these dime-store demons. The odd thing is that this same Dr. Wertham, a few years thereafter, was quite critically impressed by my first novel, *The Scarf,* and in ensuing correspondence the good doctor and I traded opinions about comic violence, just as though neither of us was aware of the murder and mayhem I perpetrated on the printed page.

But things have changed over the past half-century — things like comics, and myself. And at least some of them — the comics — have improved.

Back then it was easy to trace the roots of the story comics to the pulp magazines, from which many series characters were transported and transplanted to the paneled pages. Artwork showed the influence of newspaper comic strips, cartoons, pulp magazine illustration, and the films of the era. Much of what

those early comics offered was derivative, and some of it did, at least in part, justify the criticism of well-meaning do-gooders who feared their children would become read-badders.

And the comics were an influence, no doubt about it. Youngsters who came under that influence grew up to become influential themselves, as writers, artists, filmmakers.

Today, the influenced have become the influential, so that cause and effect have done a flip-flop. Now the comics are the innovators; newspaper art copies *their* style, and other forms of graphic art and illustration frequently adopt their techniques. And the whole "language" of modern film and television seems quite obviously translated from comics in the form of jump-cuts, enormous head shots, rapidly changing POV, and a dozen other innovations which determine emphasis and pacing — and careful editing.

All of this has been generally accepted under the convenient label of "pop art," but there are indications that talented artists, writers, and editors are starting to stretch that label. Not satisfied with endless (and frequently, mind-less) repetitions of the mixture as before, they are reaching out to broader concepts, bolder methods of reaching a more adult readership, new ways to tell old tales.

Hellboy is a brilliant example of how to elevate the comic of the future to a higher literary level while achieving a higher pitch of excitement. Its story line combines traditional concepts with modern frames of reference, the whole being swept along by a *virtuoso* treatment of dazzling artistic effects.

As in any experimental venture there are, of course, minor flaws. "Yeah, right" was not a sarcastic phrase used in 1944, nor was anyone or anything characterized as "Looney Tunes."

But these are quibbles — mere flyspecks on the dome of the Sistine Chapel. The total effect of *Hellboy* is that of a true work of art — original and innovative and exciting. Again and again you'll find panels and pages which display a sophisticated and sometimes deliberately satirized awareness of classic modes and content. The product of superb talents, they could be framed and stand forth on their own. Striking use of color enhances their effect and complements the impact of plot and scripting.

This is far from the "pop art" of the Andy Warhol world or the inane imagery of the drug culture. The creative approach found in *Hellboy* is a newly evolving art form of its own, addressed and attuned to today.

Besides, it's a killer read!

For Jack Kirby, H. P. Lovecraft,
my lovely wife Christine, and
the amazing Elmer Newton.

CHAPTER ONE

Journal of 1st Sgt.
George Whitman, USA
12/23/44
East Bromwich, England.

We've been here for
two days now and it
isn't getting any better.
All of the men are jit-
tery in this place.
Maybe if it had a name.
Maybe if the people in
the village would even
talk about it. But they
won't.

Not even telling them
there could be a crack
team of Nazi commandos
lurking about some-
wheres gets anything
out of them. They just
look at you like Nazis
are maybe the last thing
in the world they need
to worry about.
If that were true, we
wouldn't be here.
Okay--this is what we
think we know: Hitler
has sent some kind of
team to England. I
called them commandos,
but there's a trio of people from the British
Paranormal Society who
say they're more than
that. They say the
Germans are some kind of
spook squad. That the
krauts are here to per-
form some kind of spell
or something. Summon
monsters. Raise the dead.
Yeah, right.

But whatever it is, it's got the top brass worried enough to send a special Ranger unit to look into it. And the Torch of Liberty is here with us. Funny to see him standing there, having a cup of joe with the rest of the guys. I'm more used to seeing him jumping around in newsreels, fighting some cockamamie Nazi menace.

Seems like an O.K. guy, though. And he believes this whole business. He says his own sources confirm the Nazis are in the final stages of something called "Project Ragna Rok".

I don't think our Limey friends were too thrilled to learn it took the Torch's word to make us believe them.

There's three of them: Professor Malcolm Frost, from Blackfriar's College, stateside.

Trevor Bruttenholm (pronounced "Broom") who's some kind of para-normal Whiz Kid.

And Lady Cynthia Eden-Jones, who's sup-posed to be England's top medium.

And in charge of this whole Looney Toon party is me, a guy who'd never even heard the word "paranormal" before a week ago.

Anyway, two days camped out in this holi-day camp and so far nothing. No spooks. No monsters. No Nazis.

But Lady Cynthia says it's going to hap-pen here. And it's going to happen tonight.

DEAD.

AND YET... IT ISN'T. FOR AS LONG AS I CAN REMEMBER, TREVOR BRUTTENHOLM HAS BEEN LIKE A *FATHER* TO ME.

IT'S GOOD TO SEE YOU *ALIVE*, SIR.

TO SEE HIM LIKE THIS, A *SHADOW* OF THE MAN HE WAS THE LAST TIME I SAW HIM...

YOU CAME.

THANK YOU.

IT MAKES ME FEEL SOMEHOW LIKE IT MIGHT HAVE BEEN *BETTER* IF HE *HAD* DIED...

CLICK

THERE IS SOMETHING I MUST TELL YOU, HELLBOY.

SOMETHING VERY IMPORTANT.

TAKE IT *EASY*, SIR. SLOW AND EASY. LIKE YOU *TAUGHT* ME. LET IT COME AT ITS OWN PACE.

BUT... I CAN'T REMEMBER. I CAN'T...

I TALK TO HIM CALMLY, STEADILY, LIKE THERE'S NOTHING TO WORRY ABOUT.

LIKE THE LOOK ON HIS FACE DOESN'T SEND COLD SHUDDERS UP AND DOWN MY SPINE.

FINALLY...

...THE EXPEDITION...

"AND THERE, SQUATTING IN THE DARKNESS, PART OF THE DARKNESS, PART OF THE SILENCE, THE AGE...

"AND SEATED IN FRONT OF IT, SURROUNDED BY IT, ALMOST AS THOUGH IT WERE *PART* OF IT...

"YOU REMEMBER... I SHOWED YOU PICTURES OF THE STATUES FOUND ON KOFU IN THE THIRTIES. IT WAS LIKE THEM, BUT *BIGGER*. A HUNDRED TIMES BIGGER.

"HUMAN IN FORM COLD. FROZEN. SUCH EXQUISITE *DETAIL* IN THE *CARVING*.

"ALMOST LIKE SOMETHING...

"...ALIVE..."

AND WHEN I GET ANGRY I SOMETIMES DO **STUPID** THINGS.

THINGS LIKE CHARGING **HEADLONG** INTO A **PITCH BLACK ROOM.**

I'M **TOUGHER** AND **STRONGER** THAN ANY HUMAN...

...BUT I CAN'T **SEE** ANY BETTER IN THE DARK.

I WISH I COULD.

OOF!

GACK!

I STUMBLE BACK DOWN THE HALL AND MAKE A CALL TO THE *HEAD OFFICE.*

TO THE BUREAU OF PARANORMAL RESEARCH AND DEFENSE.

DOCTOR MANNING, HELLBOY IS ON LINE SEVEN.

HELLBOY! ARE YOU ALL RIGHT?

YEAH, I'M OKAY. I'M STILL IN BROOKLYN.

NO, HE'S *DEAD.* SOMETHING WAS *HERE.* SOMETHING THAT WASN'T *HUMAN.*

NO, I CAN'T EVEN *GUESS* WHAT IT WAS.

YOU BETTER SEND IN SOME OF THE LAB GUYS. LET THEM FIGURE IT OUT.

RIGHT. YES. OF COURSE. YOU'RE FREE TO ASSEMBLE YOUR OWN *TEAM,* AS ALWAYS.

AND... HELLBOY...

I'M... SORRY ABOUT PROFESSOR BRUTTENHOLM. I KNOW HOW *CLOSE* YOU WERE.

YES. GOOD-BYE.

WELL, GENTLE-MEN...

VON KRUPT, KLAUS WERNER
(Photo taken 12/2/45) Committed to
Eisenvalt Sanitarium. Died 6
months later. Body discovered to
be infested with beetles of unknown species. No explanation.

To the best determination of the assigned in-
vestigative team, "Ragna Rok" was one of
Hitler's many "Doomsday" projects initiated in
the closing days of World War Two.

Principally there were known to be five
individuals (see photos below) involved at key
steps of the project, and so far as has been de-
termined all five were present in the final mo-
ments. The project was apparently headed by
General Klaus Werner von Krupt (see addendum
under photo.)

The culmination of several years' work by
the individuals, the ritual performed on
Tarmagant Island (see map, pg. 162) on 23 Dec.
1944 corresponds precisely with the manifesta-
tion of the creature now code named "Hellboy"
(see File #25891), the so-called "HELLBOY INCI-
DENT."

Professor Trevor Bruttenholm and his
staff have examined both "Hellboy" and the
site on Tarmagant Island extensively, and al-
though no physical evidence can be found to
link the events it seems unlikely their tempo-
ral juxtaposition is merely a coincidence.

Leopold Kurtz
(b 10/11/15)
whereabouts unknown

Ilsa Haupstein
(b 6/7/19)
whereabouts unknown

Professor Doctor Karl
Ruprect Kroenen
(b unknown)
whereabouts unknown

Name Unknown
(b unknown)
whereabouts unknown

B.P. R.D.

FROGS

Frogs, like snakes, scorpions, ravens, and black cats, are traditionally considered harbingers of doom, witnessed by the following tale.

AN AFRICAN MYTH ABOUT A FROG

ON A DAY when little water was to be found, Man spent awhile in thought and realized that he might one day die, never to rise again. Man sent Dog to God to ask that he might come back to life again, like the flowering plant, after death.

Dog went off and followed his nose toward God. He was soon distracted by the smell of soup, and followed his hunger toward the source. Leaning close to watch it boil, Dog was content and forgot his mission.

Seeing that Dog was lost, Frog took it upon himself to go to God and tell him that Man did not want to live again. If Man were to be reborn, thought Frog, he would soon muddy the rivers and destroy the birthplaces of frogs.

Dog finally arrived to tell God Man's message. Leaning low, he crooned Man's need for rebirth in the song of his howl. God was touched by the devotion of Dog for Man.

But God granted the frog's wish, because he got there first.

CHAPTER TWO

I DID MY HOMEWORK BEFORE WE CAME OUT HERE.

THE HOUSE IS CALLED *CAVENDISH HALL*. IT WAS BUILT ABOUT A HUNDRED AND FIFTY YEARS AGO BY THE FIRST OF THE CAVENDISH FAMILY TO COME TO AMERICA.

BACK THEN IT STOOD ON A HIGH PROMONTORY COMMANDING A WIDE VIEW OF THE LAKE AND ALL THE LAND AROUND AS FAR AS THE HORIZON.

THESE DAYS IT'S WELL ON ITS WAY TO HAVING A SWIMMING POOL FOR A BASEMENT. IT'S BEEN SINKING SINCE THE DAY IT WAS FINISHED.

OH. DID I MENTION THERE'S SUPPOSED TO BE A *CURSE* ON THE PLACE? NOT THE HOUSE ITSELF. THE LAND. THE LAKE.

THE LOCAL INDIANS KEPT WELL CLEAR OF THIS AREA FOR A COUPLE OF THOUSAND YEARS BEFORE THE CAVENDISH FAMILY ARRIVED.

YOU MAY THINK CURSES ARE JUST SO MUCH EYEWASH, BUT I DON'T. I'VE SEEN TOO MUCH THAT MAKES ME THINK OTHERWISE.

WAY TOO MUCH.

DOES IT? I REALLY WOULDN'T KNOW.

IT HAS ALWAYS SEEMED PERFECTLY *NATURAL* TO ME. IN ALL MY LIFE I HAVE NEVER KNOWN ANY OTHER WAY.

OUR FAMILY FORTUNE WAS FOUNDED IN EUROPE, BY *ELIHU CAVENDISH.* HE BEGAN AS A SIMPLE *WHALER.* BY THE TIME HE *DIED,* HE HAD BEEN *MASTER* OF MANY GREAT SHIPS.

"BUT HE WAS NEVER AT REST, NEVER *SATISFIED.*

"HIS TRAVELS HAD TAKEN HIM AROUND THE WORLD AND BACK TWO DOZEN TIMES.

"IN STRANGE PORTS HE LEARNED... STRANGE THINGS. "

FINALLY HIS TRAVELS BROUGHT HIM TO AMERICA, AND HERE HE BUILT THIS HOUSE. THIS *CURSED* HOUSE.

HE CHOSE THIS LOCATION WITH GREAT *CARE.* NO ONE KNOWS *WHY.*

"WITH THE HOUSE COMPLETED, HE SET ABOUT PREPARING AN EXPEDITION TO THE FARTHEST REACHES OF THE ARCTIC. TO SEARCH FOR SOMETHING. SOMETHING HE LEARNED OF FROM A SCRAP OF ANCIENT PARCHMENT HE HAD ACQUIRED IN SOME LOST CORNER OF THE WORLD.

"BEFORE HE COULD LEAVE HE DIED OF TYPHUS. HE WAS ONE OF *THOUSANDS* WHO DIED THAT YEAR. "

UNFORTUNATELY, IT SEEMS MY FROGGY FRIEND IS TOUGH ENOUGH TO *TAKE* WHATEVER I HAND OUT.

I BOUNCE OFF THE VAULTED CEILING LIKE A SACK OF WET CEMENT.

A PIECE OF MY BRAIN REGISTERS THE *DAMAGE* TO THE FINE OLD ARCHITECTURE.

IT'S MY LAST *CALM* THOUGHT FOR A WHILE.

I LAND ON MY FEET.

AND I LAND *MAD*.

KRAK

AND JUST ABOUT THEN I REALIZE ABE HAS BEEN GONE WAY TOO LONG...

HELLBOY WAS RIGHT ABOUT THE FOUNDATION. I FOUND A WAY THROUGH EASILY. IT'S AMAZING THE OLD HOUSE IS STILL STANDING, THE LOWER WALLS ARE SO FULL OF HOLES.

THE WATER IS DARKER THAN ANY I'VE EVER SWUM IN BE-FORE. IT SEEMS ALMOST TO CLING TO MY SKIN, LIKE INK, LIKE OIL.

AND THERE IS NOTHING AT ALL *ALIVE* DOWN HERE. NO *ANIMALS*. NO *FISH*. NOT EVEN *ALGAE*.

A PLACE OF *DEATH.*

OLD DEATH.

AND AS I REACH THE SURFACE, I BEGIN TO THINK...

CHAPTER THREE

WHEN I LOOK BACK ON ALL THE YEARS OF MY CAREER AS THE WORLD'S GREATEST PARANORMAL INVESTIGATOR, IT SEEMS AS THOUGH I'VE SPENT A LOT OF TIME WITH BOTH FEET OFF THE GROUND.

LEAPING. FALLING. SOMETIMES BEING PICKED UP AND HURLED. I'VE SORT OF GOTTEN USED TO IT, IN FACT.

BUT THIS IS DIFFERENT. I WAS PULLED DOWN THROUGH THE FLOOR OF THE OLD *CAVENDISH* MANSION, AND IT SEEMS NOW LIKE THAT WAS HOURS AGO. DAYS AGO.

I HIT WATER AND THE PIECE OF MY BRAIN THAT'S STILL WORKING TELLS ME THAT MEANS I CAN'T HAVE FALLEN NEARLY AS FAR AS IT SEEMED.

THE CAVENDISH HOUSE SITS ON A SHALLOW SPIT OF LAND STICKING OUT INTO A LAKE. IT'S ALMOST AT THE SAME LEVEL AS THE WATER.

THE LAKE IS ONLY A FEW DOZEN FEET ABOVE SEA LEVEL, AND SINCE NO WATER CAN BE *LOWER* THAN SEA LEVEL...

...THIS BIG, DARK, COLD POOL CAN'T BE MORE THAN FIFTY OR SIXTY FEET BELOW THE HOUSE.

AS ALL THIS RUNS THROUGH MY MIND I CAN ALMOST HEAR *LIZ* CHIDING ME.

"COME ON, MR. WIZARD," SHE'D SAY, "THERE'S WORK TO BE DONE."

BUT I DON'T REALLY HEAR HER. LIZ IS GONE, SNATCHED FROM HER ROOM BY SOME UNKNOWN FORCE.

THE SAME FORCE, I'D BET, THAT PULLED ME DOWN HERE.

IT FEELS *BAD* DOWN HERE. ALL OVER MY BODY COARSE, BLACK LITTLE HAIRS RISE AND BRISTLE AT THE TOUCH OF *EVIL*.

AND THEN I HEAR THE VOICE. THE STRANGE, *FAMILIAR* VOICE...

WHAT YOU FEEL, CREATURE, IS THE LONG AND *BLOODY* HISTORY OF THIS PLACE.

OPEN YOUR SMALL MIND TO IT. CAN YOU HEAR THE *SCREAMS* OF FUTILE SACRIFICE? CAN YOU SMELL THE HOT BLOOD ON THESE COLD STONES?

EIGHT HUNDRED YEARS AGO MEN STILL WORSHIPPED THE *SERPENT* AND SOUGHT TO APPEASE HIM WITH THE BLOOD OF INNOCENTS.

FOOLS!

EIGHT CENTURIES AGO MORTALS LACKED THE *POWER* TO FREE THE BEAST.

BUT THAT POWER EXISTS NOW, HERE.

IN *ME!*

THE SERPENT CARES NOT FOR THE BLOOD OF MEN. HE CRAVES BUT ONE THING, AND THAT IS *FREEDOM*.

HE DOESN'T UTTER SO MUCH AS A *SQUEAK*, BUT THE *AIR* RINGS LIKE SOME GREAT FROZEN BELL...

...AND I FEEL FOR ALL THE WORLD LIKE SOMEBODY JUST SWATTED ME WITH A SUBMARINE.

I HIT HARD. HARD ENOUGH TO KNOCK THE WIND OUT OF EVEN ME.

NEVER AGAIN RAISE A HAND TO ME, CREATURE.

I *CONJURED* YOU INTO THIS WORLD, AND I CAN *WIPE* YOU FROM IT.

I'M BEGINNING TO BELIEVE HIM.

I'VE BEEN A PARANORMAL INVESTIGATOR GETTING ON FORTY YEARS NOW. I'VE SEEN A LOT OF THINGS. LEARNED A LOT OF THINGS.

THE POCKETS OF MY OLD COAT ARE FULL OF CHARMS AND TALISMANS I'VE COLLECTED FROM THE FOUR CORNERS OF THE WORLD.

BY RIGHTS ANY ONE OF THEM SHOULD HAVE PROTECTED ME FROM JUST ABOUT ANYTHING.

BUT EITHER HE'S *NEUTRALIZED* ALL OF THEM SOMEHOW OR--WORSE--HE'S JUST TOO DAMN POWERFUL FOR THEM TO WORK AGAINST HIM.

NICE TRICK, PUTTING YOUR HEAD BACK TOGETHER.

UNTIL I KNOW *WHICH*, I DECIDE TO *STALL* THINGS A LITTLE BIT.

...AND IF GOD CHOOSE
I SHALL BUT LOVE THEE BETTER
AFTER DEATH

AND HERE, PERHAPS, I'VE FOUND THE **CULPRITS**.

THIS PLACE OF DEATH IS NOT **ENTIRELY** WITHOUT LIFE.

THE PART OF MY BRAIN THAT'S STILL WORKING ON SOMETHING LIKE A RATIONAL LEVEL TELLS ME I'M GOING TO HAVE TO FIND A WAY TO CALL A HALT TO THIS FRACAS PRETTY SOON.

EVEN IF IT'S JUST A *SHORT* HALT. I NEED TIME TO CATCH MY SECOND WIND BEFORE FROGGY REACHES DOWN MY THROAT AND PULLS MY LUNGS OUT.

FROGGY, HOWEVER, HAS NO INTENTION OF GIVING ME THE SPACE I NEED.

I CLING TO THE SMALL HOPE THAT HE'S OPERATING SOLELY ON SOME KIND OF AMPHIBIOUS ADRENALINE.

THAT HE DOESN'T HAVE A REALLY *CLEAR* IDEA OF JUST HOW CLOSE HE IS TO *WINNING.*

SOME
HOPE.

THERE I WAS INTRODUCED TO A SMALL, DOOMED MADMAN.

BUT A MADMAN IN WHOSE DOOM I SAW A CHANCE TO HARNESS *UNLIMITED RESOURCES.*

I PERMITTED MYSELF TO BE JOINED WITH THOSE PUNY MINDS THE *REICH* HAD ASSEMBLED FOR ITSELF, BELIEVING THEM *UNEQUALED* IN THE WORLD, UNEQUALED IN THEIR TALENTS FOR CREATING WEAPONS OF *MASS DESTRUCTION.*

THEY WERE FOOLS, OF COURSE, COMPARED TO ME, BUT I SAW IN THEM ROUGH GEMS I MIGHT SHAPE AND POLISH. CRUDE THEIR THOUGHTS AND MINDS MIGHT BE...

...BUT ALSO UTTERLY *UNTARNISHED* BY THE LIMITATIONS OF *CONSCIENCE* AND *MORALITY.*

I WORKED CLOSELY WITH THE THREE I DEEMED MOST *RATIONAL* AMONG THEM. I GUIDED THEM, SO THAT IN TIME THEY THOUGHT THEY HAD THEMSELVES CONCEIVED THE PROJECT THEY NAMED *RAGNA ROK.*

HAD THEMSELVES *IMAGINED* THE CONSTRUCTION OF THE *RAGNA ROK ENGINE.*

BEHIND THEIR BACKS I *LAUGHED* AT THEIR RIDICULOUS CONCEITS. NO MERE HUMAN MIND COULD EVEN HAVE CONCEIVED SUCH A WONDROUS DEVICE, AS NO MERE HUMAN FORM COULD EVEN CONTAIN THE FORCES WHICH THE ENGINE WOULD SUMMON, MAGNIFY AND DIRECT.

DIRECT INTO *ME,* SO THAT I MIGHT BECOME THE *KEY* BY WHICH THE BEAST WOULD BE AT LAST RELEASED FROM THEIR PRIMEVAL PRISON.

AS THE THOUSAND-YEAR REICH GROUND DOWN TO ITS LAST, BITTER, BLOODY DAYS, THE PROJECT NEARED ITS CULMINATION.

ASTROLOGY GUIDED ME TO THE *PLACE.*

NUMEROLOGY GUIDED ME TO THE *TIME.*

THERE WAS NO MEANS BY WHICH THE *RESULT* OF THE EXPERIMENT COULD BE ACCURATELY PREDICTED.

I KNEW BETTER.

I DID NOT KNOW PRECISELY *WHAT,* BUT I KNEW *SOMETHING* HAD BEEN CONJURED FORTH FROM THE WORLDS BEYOND.

YOU.

THE NAZIS THOUGHT IT *FAILED.*

BUT BEFORE I COULD PRESS MY INVESTIGATION FURTHER, THE TIDE OF WAR TURNED IRREVOCABLY.

GERMANY WAS DESTROYED, HITLER, HIMMLER, ALL THE REST WERE *DEAD.*

AS TRIUMPHANT FOREIGN ARMIES MARCHED OVER THE ASHES OF THE FATHERLAND, MY BRAVE ASSOCIATES FLED TO PREARRANGED HIDING PLACES.

I WAS *ALONE.*

AND FOR THE *FIRST TIME...* I WAS *UNSURE.*

AND IT WAS THEN, AS IF MY MOMENT-ARY WEAKNESS HAD SOMEHOW REKINDLED THEM...

...THAT I HEARD ONCE MORE THE LONG SILENT *VOICES.*

THEY SPOKE, AND THEY BADE ME *GO,*

THEY BADE ME GO *NORTH.*

NORTH, TO THE ARCTIC WASTES.

TO THE VERY *TOP* OF THE *WORLD.*

WITH A HANDFUL OF PAID COMPANIONS, I MARCHED UP OVER THE BROAD SHOULDER OF THE WORLD, NORTH AND EVER NORTH.

THOSE WHO MARCHED WITH ME HAD NO INTEREST IN MY MISSION. THEY CAME ONLY FOR THE *GOLD* I PROMISED.

THEIR SOULS WERE SMALL, BUT THEY WERE SUFFICIENT TO SUSTAIN ME.

SO IT WAS *ALONE* THAT I ARRIVED AT LAST AT MY DESTINATION.

SO IT WAS MY EYES ALONE WHICH LOOKED UPON THE FABLED TEMPLE OF THE *OGDRU-JAHAD*, BUILT UNCOUNTED EONS PAST BY THE FIRST RACE OF MEN.

AND *WITHIN* ITS FROZEN WALLS, SOMETHING OLDER STILL, FOR THE TEMPLE WAS BUILT TO *CONTAIN* IT.

THE *SADU-HEM*, LEFT BY THE OGDRU-JAHAD THAT THEY MIGHT ALWAYS HAVE A FOOTHOLD IN THE WORLD FROM WHICH THEY WERE FOREVER BANISHED.

HIDDEN FROM THE EYES OF GOD, DEAD AND FOSSILIZED, TO ANOTHER IT WOULD HAVE SEEMED BUT A GROTESQUE STATUE.

BUT NOT TO ME.

I FELT ITS MIND, ALIVE AND WAITING.

SEATING MYSELF AT THE FOOT OF THE LIVING STATUE, I SENT MY BODY INTO A TRANCE, THAT MY MIND MIGHT REACH OUT TO THE SHADOW OF LIFE DEEP WITHIN ITS STONY COILS.

CHAPTER FOUR

IN FIFTY YEARS I'VE NEVER FELT LIKE THIS. NUMB, DEAD, EMPTY.

AND FILLING THAT EMPTINESS I HEAR THE WIZARD DRONE ON AND ON...

STRANGE, MAD WORDS, YET WORDS I FIND SOMEHOW *FAMILIAR*.

WORDS THAT ARE *MINGLED* WITH MY FIRST MEMORIES ON *EARTH*...

CHAINED IN HEAVEN ARE THEY, SEVEN IS THEIR NUMBER, BRED IN THE DEPTHS OF OCEAN, NEITHER MALE NOR FEMALE ARE THEY, THEY ARE AS THE HOWLING WIND, WHICH KNOWETH NOT MERCY, WHICH KNOWETH NOT PITY.

NUNN-JAHAD!

HEEDLESS ARE THEY TO PRAYER AND SUPPLICATION, THEY ARE THE SERPENT, THEY ARE THE FURIOUS BEAST, THE WINDSTORM.

ADAD-JAHAD!

EVIL WINDS THEY ARE, THE EVIL BREATH THAT HERALDETH THE BANEFUL STORM... THEY ARE MIGHTY CHILDREN, HERALDS OF PESTILENCE, THRONE BEARERS OF ERESHIGAL, WHO IS QUEEN AND LORD OVER THE GREAT DARKNESS BETWEEN WORLDS!

AMON-JAHAD!

THEY ARE THE FLOOD WHICH RUSHETH THROUGH THE LAND, SEVEN GODS OF MIGHT, SEVEN DEMONS OF OPPRESSION, SEVEN IN HEAVEN AND SEVEN ON EARTH.

IRRA-JAHAD!

ABE!

BUT...

...NOT ALONE.

IN SOME KIND OF TRANCE.

AND BEHIND HIM...

...THE SHADOWS SPEAK...

WAKE UP, GIRL

THE WIZARD *MOCKED* THE SCIENTISTS WHO TRIED TO UNDERSTAND THE POWER LOCKED UP INSIDE LIZ SHERMAN.

HE THOUGHT HE KNEW BETTER THAN THEM. THOUGHT HE COULD REACH DOWN INSIDE HER AND PULL OUT JUST AS MUCH OF THAT POWER AS HE NEEDED.

PITY.

IF HE'D ONLY *ASKED* ME, I COULD HAVE TOLD HIM HE WAS *WRONG.*

WHAT A *MESS!*

YOU'LL HAVE TO LET ME READ YOUR *REPORT* ON THIS ONE, HELLBOY...

...ASSUMING WE GET OUT SO YOU CAN *WRITE* IT.

DEAL.

THERE'S A LOT MORE CONFIDENCE IN MY VOICE THAN THERE IS IN MY HEART.

ALL AROUND US THE OLD STONES OF CAVENDISH HOUSE ARE GIVING UP THEIR LONG WAR WITH GRAVITY.

STATUARY A MUSEUM CURATOR WOULD GIVE YEARS OFF HIS LIFE TO POSSESS RAINS DOWN INTO THE CAULDRON THAT USED TO BE SADU-HEM.

I WONDER IF THE CREATURE IS STILL ALIVE ENOUGH TO FEEL THE PAIN OF THE STONE AND THE FIRE.

I HOPE SO.

MOVE! MOVE!! MOVE!!!

I DON'T REMEMBER TOO MUCH OF IT, HELLBOY.

I WAS LOOKING AT WHAT I THOUGHT WAS A *STATUE* OF OLD ELIHU CAVENDISH...

...AND THEN THERE WAS A *HARPOON* STICKING THROUGH A GUY...

AND THERE WAS A REALLY BIG MONSTER...

IMAGINE MY *CONFUSION*.

AND WHEN EVERYTHING CAUGHT FIRE...

I DIDN'T KNOW WHAT THE HELL WAS GOING ON!

SOUNDS TO ME LIKE OLD MAN CAVENDISH TOOK OVER YOUR BODY, ABE.

HE WAS THE ONE WHO DID THE HARPOONING.

YES, YOUR "MR. RAGNA ROK" KILLED THE *LAST* OF ELIHU'S FAMILY, AN OLD FAMILY WITH A LOT OF *PAIN* ATTACHED TO ITS NAME,

ENOUGH TO ALLOW HIM TO REACH FROM BEYOND THE GRAVE TO EXTRACT HIS *VENGEANCE.*

MM.

OR MAYBE HE WAS JUST *PISSED* BECAUSE SOMEBODY ELSE FOUND THAT THING UP IN THE ARCTIC BEFORE HIS PEOPLE DID.

THEY SPENT A LONG TIME LOOKING. WE DON'T KNOW THINGS WOULD HAVE BEEN ANY DIFFERENT IF THEY'D FOUND SADU-HEM.

WHAT ABOUT YOU, LIZ? THAT OLD WIZARD HAD YOU *ZONKED* PRETTY GOOD. DO YOU REMEMBER ANY MORE THAN ABE DOES?

A LITTLE, NOT MUCH.

BEEP

BEEEP

BEEEEEEEEEEEEEEE.....

WHERE THE HELL DID HE COME FROM?

Personal reminiscences by Mike Mignola.

LEFT: This is a drawing done for a convention program book — I added the name Hellboy at the last minute and it made me laugh. The name stuck and the character started to take shape in my head.

BELOW: I first envisioned *Hellboy* as a team book, but I couldn't come up with a name for any of the other characters or the team. Hellboy's in the process of mutating from that first drawing into the guy we know and love today — look at the size of his neck!

RIGHT: Hellboy in his final form. I originally intended this piece to be a promotional poster for the first *Hellboy* miniseries but I wasn't happy with Hellboy's right hand.

HELLBOY

©MIGNOLA
93

MORE FIRST THINGS—

THE following stories are the first Hellboy stories ever produced, done to promote the miniseries and introduce the character. The first story ran in *San Diego Comic-Con Comics* #2, given away at the 1993 San Diego Comic Con. The second story was published in the *Comics Buyer's Guide.*

I wasn't much concerned with plot, but I did learn a couple of things — Hellboy looks better with a coat, and I like to draw gorillas with big bolts sticking out of them.

The art on this page is the first Hellboy promotional piece, and the first appearance of his coat.

CURIOUS JUXTAPOSITION. I'VE BEEN AROUND THE WORLD AND BACK A FEW TIMES IN MY DAY, BUT I'VE NEVER SEEN ANYTHING QUITE LIKE *THIS*.

A BIG COWBOY BOOT. AND AN EGYPTIAN SCARAB BEETLE. AND A SWASTIKA.

TOO MANY *IDIOMS*, IF YOU ASK ME.

ONLY THERE'S NOBODY HERE TO ASK ME.

IN THE PAST COUPLE OF YEARS A WHOLE FLOCK OF SMALL TOWNS HAVE *DRIED UP* DOWN AROUND THESE PARTS.

PEOPLE VANISHED WITHOUT A TRACE. NO SIGN OF *VIOLENCE*. JUST--*GONE*.

THIS TOWN IS THE LATEST. AND THE FIRST TO COME TO MY ATTENTION.

HUH?

A DOG?

A DOG. KIND OF A MANGY LITTLE MUTT. LOOKS *HUNGRY*, TOO.

MUST HAVE BEEN HERE ON HIS OWN SINCE EVERYBODY VANISHED.

HEY, PUP! DON'T BE AFRAID.

I'M NOT NEARLY AS *SCARY* AS I...

...LOOK...

HELLBOY ™

G A L L E R Y

featuring

SIMON BISLEY
colored by Matthew Hollingsworth

MIKE ALLRED

ART ADAMS
colored by Matthew Hollingsworth

FRANK MILLER

FRED BLANCHARD

and

GARY GIANNI

ARTHUR ADAMS